If I Die, Here's What I Meant

Ryan Truax

ISBN: 978-1-7356185-1-7

Prologue

~*To My Mother:*

Our connection continues to pierce through the chasm that separates us.
You are the love of my life, Mom. I hope that you can read this in heaven.
I pray that once you finish reading this book, you will turn and look to God with pride.
I have less to say to you than I do to Dad, because you and I got to say it all.
I miss you so, so, so much. I am trying to make it down here without you.
There are days I believe will be my last. I'm having a really hard time, Mama.
However, every morning I wake up, I know it's because God has sanctioned it.
And if God has sanctioned it, then it must be for His glory.
And if it is for His glory, may I consider it pure joy when I face trials of many kinds.
Therefore, I won't ever stop trying for as long as He keeps me here.
When you were dying, you continued to apologize.
As I said then, I continue to say now: You have nothing to be sorry for.
I owe you everything. I am filled with gratitude. Thank you, Mama. I love you.

~*To My Father:*

Dad, you've been gone for almost 18 years. I lost Mom less than 2 years ago.
I already have more closure with her departure than I can ever fathom having with yours.
As a child, I had a faint idea of who you were in my naive, developing young mind.
As a man, I've clung to the stories your friends have given to me in small and seldom doses.
In vain, I futilely try to piece each one together until they reveal to me who you were.
I'll never accumulate enough pieces in this lifetime to show me the shape of your soul.
I am in so much pain because I know it was so beautiful, and I will never get to see it, Dad.
I used to wonder why I was so angry at you. Now, I understand: I am so angry that I lost you.
I will never be able to make the connection between our last conversation and your departure.
Daddy, I just so desperately thirst for your approval. My spirit is so dehydrated.
I hope you didn't leave because of me? I hope that I was good enough for you.

My soul is in denial that you're gone. I dream of you year after year, hoping you'll come back.
And while I know that you can't, I pray that you will read this book.
I pray that you will know the man that I became, even though I will never know the man
that you were when you were here. I miss you. I love you. I believed in you.
May the void of your absence finally be filled when I get to heaven.
They always told me that I'd eventually forget what your voice sounded like.
But I remember the way you sounded perfectly.
No number of years can silence your voice.
Now, I am using mine.
This is for you, Dad.

~To The Underdogs:

They're gonna laugh at you for dreaming.
They might even be your own parents.
But if you have a desire and a passion-
and if you dream of achieving something obsessively-
You can bring that goal to fruition.
Work very hard.
It's not over.

~To Everyone:

I've wanted to write this
since I was nine years old.
My parents always believed in it
and I'm heartbroken that
they are unable to see it
finally come to fruition.
This book is dedicated
to my Mom and Dad.
Without their fiery spirits,

I'd have never burned inside
enough to chase my dreams.

This book is a raw collection of thoughts.
May you deeply connect with my heart.
Thank you endlessly for reading this.

Lastly, every single word
from the first to last page
is written about true experiences,
my actual past, my actual life,
and real, actual people.
Their names and identities
have been changed
to protect their privacy,
but what you're about to read
is a factual journal
about factual people.
My journal. My life.
My past. My present.
My triumphs. My failures.
My pain. My faith.
My sin. My repentance.
My everything.
I put my entire heart into this.
May it in some way encourage you.

And so, if I die, here's what I meant.

—Ry

All glory to God.

Contents

Love

I don't need you to touch yourself up.
I want you raw and unedited.

You just need to unlearn all of
the negative things he spoke over you.

May the rain that falls upon us
make our eyes close tighter while we kiss.

My favorite time to look at you
is the moment that you wake up.

When I lack stillness and understanding,
the answers rest in the scent of your skin.

There's no one else's hair
I'd rather tuck behind one ear
to expose a pretty jawline
as I lean in to boldly kiss
than you.

The images that bring
my restless mind to sleep
are of you and I together.
Dreaming of you calms my soul.

Your hands feel like high heaven
to the depths of my anxious soul.
Your fingertips extract me out of hell.
Please, please continue to touch me.

If you love me enough to kiss me so hard
that you cut your lips on my teeth,
I'll love you enough to cut to the chase
and be yours forever.

We looked out the window of your apartment,
and we saw ourselves exploring the world.
So, you grabbed your keys and we left.

Remember My Poems

In 5th grade, you'd write me letters.
You'd have your friend pass them to me
when we would sit around in class.
I never knew how to react.
I couldn't receive your affirmations.
And so, I'd rudely and foolishly avoid you.
Finally, after many unanswered writings,
you wrote me one final note.
And in it all it said was,

"Remember my poems
when you're rich and famous."

Well, it's been many years.
And, I'm not rich.
And, I'm not famous.
But I still remember
all your lovely poems.
The irony here is this:
You wrote about
what you thought
I was worthy of.
But true worth is
what cannot ever
be forgotten.
And I remember
all your letters.

I remember your poems.

K

I'll never forget
hiking and running up hills with you
all afternoon on the trails of Griffith Park
sitting together on the rocks up at the top.
In one way was the 134 freeway and Burbank
in another way was the Hollywood sign
in another way was downtown Los Angeles
in the final way was Santa Monica and the ocean.
We prayed and held each other and wept.
You could pray unlike anyone I ever heard.
Your eyes would close so tight.
I'll never forget
going to see you in the hospital after church.
You swore I didn't have to come
though, naturally, I did regardless.
I was greeted by your Mother.
Her eyes were kind and slightly concerned.
You got your eyes from her.
She told me that only one person
was allowed to see you at a time.
She gave me her wrist band so that I could get to you.
I was struck by the trust that she had in me
having only just met me and she thanked me.
I found you in the hallway in your hospital bed.
They didn't have a room for you, and you were alone.
You had a blue hospital gown on, and you had no make-up on.
You apologized for the way you looked.
I rebuked your apology with affirmations.
We held hands and giggled for a while,

the nurse told us that we were cute,
I told you that I loved you,
you said, "God, I love you, too, Ry."
I gave the wrist band back to your Mother
as she told me she was praying for my Mom.
We embraced and then I left.
You got better, and we explored our love together.
You shared your love of painting with me.
I shared my love of drumming with you.
You shared your love of wardrobe styling with me.
I share my love of writing with you.
We'd talk about life in the middle of The Grove.
We'd talk about life in the middle of your yard.
We'd talk about life in the middle of Poinsettia.
We'd talk about life in the middle of LACMA.
I really, really loved you.
You really, really loved me, too.
The timing just was off.
I wasn't mature enough for you.
You weren't open enough for me.
You had unresolved feelings for that T.V. host.
I had unresolved issues with pornography.
We both knew we needed to separately grow.
We weren't ready to share our lives forever.
I heard you moved to New Jersey.
Maybe you heard I moved to Oregon.
But Los Angeles will always be for us.
We cried in front of your house the last time I ever saw you.
We stood on your grass in the dark for hours
while my car hummed softly in neutral.
We never got to visit your Dad back in Vermont.
We never got to build the future we both loved to dream of.

We couldn't admit what was happening.
We couldn't articulate a goodbye.
The sincerity in your bright blue eyes.
Your tears I continued to brush my cheekbones on.
The fear without you now.
Your fear without me now.
We found comfort in our terror.
We found closure in our love.
Courageously, and illogically,
we passionately embraced
with our salty tears
running down our faces
with my car running
right behind me
which was
waiting on
me
to
go.
I'll never forget.

The Whittier Girl

She lost her Dad to Cancer.
She constantly carried that pain.
Her Dad photographed rock stars.
Her Mom was an artist, too.
I never met a girl so petite yet tough.
I never knew a girl who dressed like her.
I mean, she taught me all about style.
I mean, she taught me all about rock n' roll.
She liked men who were musicians.
She liked men who could create.
She liked that I could write.
She liked that I could drum.
God ... She was so down for me.
God ... She didn't tolerate any b.s.
You know, she was an East L.A. girl.
You know, she didn't just LOOK the part.
She WAS the part that we ALL admire.
She embodied that sexy spark.
That broken-homed, ride or die chick.
That leather jacketed, in your face chick.
That cigarette smoking, pot smoking chick.
That vintage clothing-wearing chick.
But she was extremely elegant.
But she was dainty and feminine.
But she was deep inside her beauty.
But she was timeless and stunning.
She'd walk in and dudes would inhale.
She'd walk out and dudes would exhale.
She'd work hard to pay our rent.

She'd feed me dinner on our porch.
My Mother loved her, too.
Her Mother loved me, too.
Our place was in San Gabriel.
Our place was near the 10 freeway.
Yeah, I had this working-class girl.
Yeah, I loved her fiery spirit.
Flawless, white teeth.
Deep, red lipstick.
Sad, brown eyes.
Long, black hair.
Cut it short, dyed it platinum.
Her bone structure pulled it off.
Her face could pull it off.
She'd paint her toes black.
She'd also paint them white.
She'd wear tight leather pants.
She'd wear ripped Rolling Stone t-shirts.
We'd drive around and listen to The Beatles.
We'd drive around and listen to The Hives.
We'd drive around and listen to Weezer.
We'd drive around and listen to Iggy Pop.
My girl would only drink madly expensive drinks.
My girl would sip top shelf cocktails.
My girl knew all the best L.A. spots.
My girl always got in without question.
I admit, she had an attitude problem.
I admit, she had a short fuse.
I admit, she was super emotional.
I admit, she had a temper.
But all these characteristics
made for unblemished sincerity.

And all these characteristics
made for raw authenticity.
So all these characteristics
made her who she was.
Loving all these characteristics
made me a better young man.
Despite her famous ex boyfriend
always breathing down my neck,
we lived our lives like true lovers.
We were the real deal
regardless of our losses
regardless of our baggage
regardless of our pasts.
Anytime I head near the 562,
anytime I head near the 626,
I always miss the Whittier girl.

Enamorment

I'm desperate to steal you from the world.
I'm jealous of the ground you walk on.
I'll lay down and let your feet press into me.
I shake with anticipation because of you.
I look for you in crowds around the world.
I stumble from the sound of your voice.
I want to be imperfect and clumsy for you.
I'm undeserving of your acceptance.
I never had a woman clean my wounds.
I never knew you could be out there.
I admittedly hoped that you were.
I thrust my heart into your perfect hands.
Your taste is like an addiction.
Your pheromones ignite my soul.
Your lips are delightful to bite.
Your neck gets traced by my tongue.
Your salty skin after you workout is so hot.
Your breath upon my body is volcanic.
Your fingers slip across my teeth.
Your body is artwork as it lays itself down.
Your soles and arches rest on my nose.
Your scent is like a nontoxic heroin.
Your fluent movements stir me into ecstasy.
Your smile throughout it all is gorgeous.

Intimacy

Drag your lips across my face.
May your saliva seep into my skin.
May your tongue inhibit my mouth
May your pretty hand tightly clench my neck.
Drag your toes across my waist.
May your feet be pampered by the pedi that I treated you to.
May your soles be extra soft.
May your arches be extra elegant.
Drag your clothes off your gorgeous body.
May your confidence be full as you bare yourself.
May your sexual tension cause you to pour.
May your inhibitions be on the floor with your abandoned outfit.
Drag your mouth across my body.
May your teeth sink into my abs.
May your breath bring warmth to my obliques.
May your scent bring me a dizzying need to release.
Drag me into explosive oblivion - but only after I've done the same for you.

Several times - relentlessly, unpredictably, but delightfully and intensely - in a row.

Love is intimate. And intimacy is passionate.

May our passion for one another melt us like hot metal until our souls lose both their shapes.

Lessons From Enamorment And Intimacy

Men who are led by fleshly desires
inevitably self-destruct and
as they throw themselves into
their passionate, lustful inclinations,
they reap an outstanding debt
of spiritual damage
not only to themselves
but to every woman
they dishonored by
leading them into
hasty, sexual relationships.
I have been that kind of "man."
And so, dear friend, pray for me.
Pray that my love
for the moment decreases
and that my will
to abstain for His glory increases.
Lord, have mercy on me - a sinner.

Toxicity

You're taking this long to leave him
because he's convinced you
that there's nowhere else
for you to go.

That is a lie.

Simply Holding Hands

It had been years since our time together
walking around on Fairfax
near your West Hollywood apartment
& we'd hold hands on Melrose
anyway, I needed to walk
as I felt restless at home
& it was a Friday night
I turned down every invite
I turned every friend
I turned every plan
just like I always do
so that I could sit around alone
but I didn't want to sit this evening
I put on my jeans
a white t shirt
my Schott leather jacket
black shoes
and I headed out
I walked north on Wilton
then west on Franklin
passed Gelson's and
into Franklin Village
as always, it was crowded
especially being a Friday
the vintage shops
the juicery
the book store
and the Upright Citizens Brigade
which is where you were standing

right in front with your date
you looked so hot
in your leather jacket
long blonde hair
minimal makeup
so fit
so vibrant
green eyes
bright white smile
you always made me nervous
this wasn't any different
but I knew I didn't have to be
and we had five seconds together
you stopped listening
to whatever he was saying
I never even saw his face
I totally disregarded him
he was gonna have to wait
"Hi…"
"Hi…"
I touched your hand
and you squeezed mine
I squeezed yours back
your fingers were so soft
your fingers were so warm
your nails were so pretty
just like they were years ago
when we were together
but I slowly kept walking
as I felt your date's blood boil
still you didn't care
we had our five seconds

we savored it and connected
you knew it'd be our last
and I knew it too
because this moment
was just an accident
I was supposed to be home
like I always was on Friday nights
thinking of girls I used to know like you
you smiled
I smiled
it was clear that
the connection withstood the years
and for the both of us
that was the greatest way
that we could have ever ended it
simply holding hands
I vanished in the crowd
you vanished behind me for good

H-Bear

you cleaned me up
when I couldn't clean up
after my own self
& my Mom was dying
& I was out of shape
& I was out of energy
but you came to my apartment
in a dangerous neighborhood
off of Sunset and Western
abandoning an affluent Brentwood
to open yourself up
to the sexual harassment
of the weirdos who lingered
up and down my block
just so that you could
clean the mess I'd made
only to ask for
nothing in return
I knew it then
& I know it now -
you're the realest girl
the most down for me girl
the most sincere girl
I've ever, ever been with
and I know you know it's true
as you damn well should know
because you left the most
beautiful part of the city
to dwell in the darkest part of town

just because I was there
& you made me realize that
when a rich girl
follows a poor man
there's true wealth in her love
and true favor in his life
and so for that I thank you
and I love you, H Bear

Sexual Shame

I never took a girl's virginity without taking my dignity along with it.

Car Rides Across Los Angeles

Every time you'd pick me up,
you'd always have the greatest songs playing in your car.
You always wore those red converse.
You always wanted to see Los Angeles.
And we did.

Strikingly Attractive

This girl walked by in the downtown Arts District.
It was a gorgeous afternoon in Los Angeles.
My Ray-Bans concealed how thoroughly I observed her.
She was lean and fit.
She was a brunette and had dark sunglasses on, too.
Her hair was so long and so healthy.
She was covered in elegantly placed, single-needled, black and grey tattoos.
She was wearing denim shorts, a white tank top, and she was carrying a thin leather jacket.
She had subtle bracelets on. She was wearing sandals and her toes were painted black.
Never talked to her, never knew her name, never made eye contact with her.
She never knew I existed, but I'll ALWAYS remember the girl I saw in downtown L.A.

Savoring Simplicity

This.
Sunlight in your apartment.
Fresh coffee.
Your Malibu-kissed hair.
Your beautiful, deeply-arched feet on my lap.
I listen to you read poetry.
This.

Chemistry

I kissed you and our souls fell into one another.

Cute To The Core

What's the so-called "ugliest" part about you,
and why are you so hesitant
to share it with anyone?
Because, if you allow me,
I'll kiss that part of you
in any way you like.

Getting dumped does not define you.

She painted a portrait of me with her talent,
but she branded a love in me with her soul.

Vulnerability Is Very Attractive

I'd drive slowly up the street you live on.
I'd never judge your car in the driveway.
I'd absorb the pathway to your door.
I'd take off my shoes and walk it barefoot.
I'd feel the gravel of your land under me.
I'd listen to the tone of your doorbell.
I'd notice how many keyholes there are.
I'd hear your cute little feet walking to me.
I'd wait as you unlock your entryway.
I'd remain outside until you invite me in.
I'd rebuke your apology for the mess.
I'd assure you how clean your home looks.
I'd stop you from frantically picking up.
I'd stare at your paintings and photos.
I'd listen to you describe their origins.
I'd admire them NOT out of obligation.
I'd tell you they're pretty & yes I'd mean it.
I'd have a drink - whatever you're having.
I'd let you know I'm thankful you let me in.
I'd appreciate your cautious invitation.
I'd declare that you decorate wonderfully.
I'd tell you that nothing needs changing.
I'd make friends & play with your animals.
I'd empty your trash & water your flowers.
I'd ask for a tour if you would grace me.
I'd grab you by the hand as you show me.
I'd interrupt your nervous justifications.
I'd debunk all of your explanations.
I'd make sure you didn't owe me any.

I'd stare intently in your mirrors.
I'd savor every streak and blotch.
I'd love the spots that you missed.
I'd adore all that runs across them.
I'd let myself bleed if I got cut by one.
I'd procrastinate from bandaging it.
I'd never let you apologize for it.
I'd be fine not leaving here unscathed.
I'd be fine if I injured myself deep inside.
I'd hope you'd feel worth risking it for.
Your wounds could become my wounds.
My wounds could become yours, too.
We could sit inside this mess forever.
It'd all get sorted quicker together.
I don't want to leave & go back home.
I prefer to be here with you deep inside.
You could run your pretty lips across me.
Smudge your lipstick across my jawline.
I won't shy away from a so-called mess.
Softly shake as you exhale into me.
I want you raw & completely unedited.
Pull me inside & lock the door behind us.
Vulnerability is so very attractive.

Cheers Girl

I love how you're patient with my impatience
it's amazing that you're complacent with
all of my attributes I'm insecure, absolutely
my jealousy is reigning in a place that's full of sun
I've plateaued and I feel pain but despite it all, you call me number one
and I never knew a woman who could protect me like you do
I cannot emulate you, though it's all I try to do
that time you held me so long through every single song
was beyond the strongest love that which I cannot dispute
we speak the same dialect, but talk a different language
you say "elaborate," but girl, I just explained it
and though our different worlds bring the one we share anguish
It's an alliance too well put together to rearrange and
yeah there's been some changes and it's been a minute since I've seen you
so get your server to bring you something good to drink to
I'm gonna ask you to raise a glass and while you're tossin' it back to me and you
trip out that no one will have you or me like we had me and you
cheers girl

Time

Assure this,
I'd push you away
and I'd run
into whatever would hit
and know this
I am only for you
you'd live this
and live me out
for me
in that
I pulled you out
and left me in
for you
for us
for all of time

Oxygen

Love like it's oxygen.
Love like we breathe.
Love like it's involuntary.
Love like we'll suffocate without it.
Breathe it into full-lung capacity.
Love like it's oxygen.

Eye Contact Is Sexy

I'll feel your eyes build tension.
I'll study them continuously.
I'll admire their overwhelming beauty.
I'll immerse myself in your presence.
I don't need to speak at all.
I know how much we talk in silence.
I can't evade the beauty of your face.
I have to visually lose myself in you.
I'd let you destroy my heart.
I'd let you explore it with passion.
I'd let you take all the risks you want.
I'd let you be reckless and dangerous.
You're intoxicatingly potent.
You're undeniably addictive.
You're enough to keep me alive.
You're enough to make me die.
You know just how to handle me.
You may take me as you wish.
You are THE new standard.
You have this down so perfectly.
You'd be so good for me longterm.
You'd be whom I'd love to serve.
You'd be adored relentlessly, I swear.
You'd blur the lines of every boundary.
We don't need to figure it out right now.
We don't have to make any plans.
We don't know if this is already over.
We might've been done before we met.
We're not gonna know 'til we do this.

We're so invested it's insane.
We're so insane I feel enlightened.
We're exploding with raw chemistry.
We'd look so good together in photos.
We'd be seeping with love and passion.
We'd have bite marks on our bodies.
We'd tangle ourselves in each other.
I want your pretty nails to scratch me.
It's your hair - your taste & your scent.
It's your perfect teeth - your pretty hands.
It's your waste, your legs - your style.
It's your skin - your super cute toes.
I just want to touch every inch of you.
This all began when I saw you.
This all began when you saw me.
This all began with silence.
This all began with eye contact.
Your eyes are extremely sexy.

Love shouldn't feel like a chore.

If You Were A Song

I'd love your rhythm if you were a song.
I'd turn you up so insanely high.
I'd let your sound surround me.
I'd let myself drown in every note.
I'd put you on repeat over and over.
I'd savor your every melody.
I'd vibrate beneath your chords.
I'd memorize your verses.
I'd shout out every chorus.
I'd get tattoos of all your lyrics.
I'd learn how to cover your work.
I'd put a simpler spin on your music.
I'd do that 'cause I can't replicate you.
I'd be unable to duplicate your beauty.
I'd be inadequate regardless of skill.
I'd try to perform it for you, though.
I'd fill with fright as you sit down to listen.
I'd pray to God you like my version.
I'd desire to somehow inspire you.
I'd hope you'd pick up your instrument.
I'd love to play your song with you.
I'd love to make one sound with you.
I'd sing your lyrics together with you.
I'd delight in every measure with you.
I'd be distressed if the music stopped.
I'd explode if I didn't express myself.
I'd go deaf if I couldn't hear your beauty.
I'd learn you and I'd love you.
I'd never carelessly play you.
I'd always carefully listen to you.

I Miss You Even Though You're Next To Me

I love and have to watch you.
You're merely in your element.
You're simply sitting next to me.
You're good at being yourself.
You're good at building tension.
You're good at knowing I want you.
You're good at being confident.
You're good at only needing you.
You're good at wanting me anyway.
I love and have to sit with you.
Your neck and hair smells lovely.
Your pheromones are a surge of euphoria.
Your name should be Serotonin.
Your presence brings me peace.
Your personality's perfection.
Your voice is sweet and comforting.
Your face is so adorable.
I love and have to touch you.
Your bare feet are so pretty.
Your bare feet are so soft.
Your bare feet belong on my chest.
Your bare feet belong in my hands.
Let me paint your toes for you.
Let me choose the color, please.
Solid black or solid white?
Either color makes me crazy.
May I be thorough and take my time?
Relax your toes and watch me play.
Just tell me what you like the most.

I'll repeat it with extra attention.
I'd love to selfishly explore you.
I'd love to make your face turn red.
I'd love to increase your heart rate.
I'd love to show you something new.
I'd love to make you shake and sigh.
I'd love to make you feel so loved.
I love and have to tell you.
I miss you though I'm next to you.
I miss you though I've got you.
I miss you all the time it seems.
I miss you though you're with me.

I love You More Than Coffee

I've tasted coffee in San Diego.
I've tasted coffee in Orange County.
I've tasted coffee in Los Angeles.
I've tasted coffee in Sacramento.
I've tasted coffee in Portland, OR.
I've tasted coffee in Las Vegas, NV.
I've tasted coffee in Phoenix, AZ
I've tasted coffee in Burlington, VT.
I've tasted coffee in Boston, MA.
I've tasted coffee in Montreal, Quebec.
I've tasted coffee in Reykjavik, Iceland.
I've tasted coffee in Dublin, Ireland.
I've tasted coffee in Venice, Italy.
I've tasted coffee in Dubrovnik, Croatia.
I've tasted coffee in Paris, France.
I've tasted coffee in Barcelona, Spain.
I've explored the flavors of this world.
I've explored the hand-crafted roasts.
I've explored the Single Origins.
I've explored the Blends.
The Macchiatos.
The Americanos.
The Pour-Overs.
The Expressos.
The French-Presses.
The Light Roasts.
The Medium Roasts.
The Dark Roasts.
Arabica Beans.

Robusta Beans.
Liberica Beans.
Even Excelsa Beans.
And my Chemex I brew with at home.
I've tasted and explored it all.
After everywhere I have been -
After everything I have tasted -
I can say with confidence -
I can say with certainty -
I love you more than all of it.
I love you more than coffee.

You make me so nervous … & I love it.

You arrived & instantly made me nervous.
You looked so good you gave me chills.
You are unimaginably attractive to me.
You have no idea how distracted I was.
I saw your beauty and I was captivated.
I saw your pretty hair that was down.
I saw your black tank top and jeans.
I saw your sandals & white-painted toes.
We were in a room with other people.
We weren't talking to each other.
We were hanging with our own friends.
We weren't even making eye contact.
How could I concentrate with you there?
How could I pretend I didn't notice you?
How could I keep my eyes off you?
How could I control any of my thoughts?
Do you realize how gorgeous you are?
Do you know that you're so rare?
Do you think about me like this, too?
Do you understand that I was shaking??
How could I concentrate or socialize?
How could I not feel your presence?
How could I not be intoxicated by you?
How could I speak level headedly at all?
We have so much chemistry, it's insane.
We act like it doesn't vibrate the room.
We act like our lips don't belong together.
We play like this isn't consuming us both.
I wanted to talk to you SO badly, okay?

I wandered around the room like a fool.
I hung around for the right moment.
I know that you noticed me - I felt it.
You were waiting for me to talk to you.
You wanted me to approach you.
You were standing there with your friend.
You wanted me to walk up to you first.
The truth is, maybe that's all in my head.
The truth is, maybe you didn't notice me.
The truth is, maybe it's wishful thinking.
The truth is, though, if I felt it -
then you must have, too. & I love it.
You make me so nervous. & I love it.
You throw me deeply off guard. & I love it.
Don't EVER wonder if I saw you - I did.
I stole glances of you standing there.
I stole glances of your eyes & your face.
I stole glances of your hair & your outfit.
I stole glances of your cute toes & hands.
But I was too nervous to say anything.
You make me so nervous.
And I love it.

Love

The truth is,
all my love
prior to knowing Christ
is nothing but
an elaborate empire
of lustful, sulfuric soot.
Through HIS NAME ONLY
do I know -
and become capable of -
true love. I'm a work in progress.
I have - however - survived each loss.

Loss

Despite its towering size,
I will tackle the trauma.

I lost my Mom to Cancer,
but she NEVER lost her battle.
Dying is not defeat.

I have been betrayed,
but I will continue to trust.

Why Did You Have To Jump?

before now, I had total apathy
not a single way out, black dark around me
thinkin' back now as to how I happily
allowed crack and downers to surround me

before now, the suppressive
so passive aggressive, had me second guessing
so down from the oppression
the massive depression, as I'm recollecting

before now, deep with anger
bitter and careless, steep in danger
me? Self-awareness? nope, a stranger
no hope to cope did dope on the regular

before now, hooked to drugs
broken down via a broken home, so corrupt
dad would beat mom until the neighbors would come
roughing her up, cover it up, it goes on and on

first, he took pills and tried to kill himself
he lost the will, could not deal with himself
did not want to feel the real himself
would rather die and steal himself

why did you have to jump?

I remember how all the cops were called
on top of it all, they couldn't break your fall at all
I remember the bones you broke
though we never spoke you know it broke me

I remember December the seventh
you forever a contender went to heaven
I remember when you died and I called your phone
nope, nobody home so I was all alone

remember the eulogy that I wrote?
the night before at your best friend's home
life brings me a tall calamity
not a single "I'm sorry" from my so-called family

friends close to me totally closed me off
no call no nothing those punks went soft
just floored, at the morgue
holding a box of ashes and asking how are these yours

that's when Dad looked upon his will
sadly Dad took the clock off the sill
Dad had me but took off still
you think it's surreal, skeptical, well, it's real

why did you have to jump?

Soul Stuck

Dad, even though your days were numbered,
why do I feel responsible
that your number wasn't higher?
My spirit wanders for you, even though you're absent.

My soul still counts on you
as if your days have yet to cease.

Your spirit left the bridge that day,
but my spirit climbed up there to save you.
And I haven't figured out just yet
how to get it to come back down.

Precisely And Distinctly

Dad, remember the morning you died?
I napped in numbness and exhaustion.
You came to me in a dream.
You said, "Hi Ry, I'll always be watching you."

Dad, was that really God allowing you to assure me?
Or was that the wishful thinking inside me as I slept?
My favorite part of that dream was your beautiful voice.
They told me I'd forget its sound, but I still hear that dream.

Unhealthy Meditations

Dad, I listen to your favorite songs in bittersweetness.
Bitter that I cannot listen to them in your car with you.
Sweet that I can remember us doing that together.
Bitter and sweet that I feel despair and joy together.

Dad, yesterday I laid beside my drumset and my guitar.
I listened to your favorite songs over, and over, and over.
It hurt me more than it helped me, yet I continued to listen anyway.
I'd rather drown in your presence than breathe in your absence.

Drinkin' n' Thinkin' Of Dad

Dad, I took your best friend to dinner in L.A.
I grilled him with heavy-hitting questions about you until he cried.
My thirsting obsession to know you has left me completely dehydrated.
Or, maybe that was all the whiskey and honeycomb I was consuming.

The Fields Of California

Dad, I was angry at you when your body was cremated.
I didn't go to Heasley field with Mom to scatter your ashes.
Many years have passed, and I drag my fingertips in the dirt of Sierra Madre.
I stroke what's left of you; I watch small clumps of you disintegrate to where the wind is going.

Dad, how tirelessly and fruitlessly have I stood on this baseball field?
It is I, the regretful man who searches for his Father.
It is I, the arrogant man who continues to think he could have saved you.
I always stand on the pitcher's mound and I listen for you.

I never leave the field until I see the green, wild parrots you loved so much.
I fantasize that you've become one of them, and now, you guard our hometown.
I double check underneath the snack bar to make sure the plaque you left is still there.
It always is, and - in pain - I walk back down to my car with a tiny piece of serenity.

Tattoo For My Father

Dad, I finally figured it out after all these years.
It's a set of praying hands, your initials, with the words
"Jesus, please remember him," above the hands.
Like the thief on the cross said to Jesus, you know?

I went down the street to the Sunset Strip and walked into Shamrock.
My tattooer lost his Dad as well. He has many tattoos. Spiders on his chest.
To my pleasure, legendary tattooer Mark Mahoney walked in with his wife.
He talked to me about the tattoo as his colleague was inking it into my arm.

"Did your Dad achieve the success he wanted?" He asked.
"No. He could have, but he didn't," I replied.
Mark had pain in his eyes, and I knew I had pain in mine as well.
"Tattoos are like scars," he said. We shook hands and we understood each other.

Day Terrors Of Being Fatherless

Dad, remember the night terrors and sleep paralysis I'd get as a child?
You'd nervously laugh as you'd try to snap me out of it.
I miss those days, and I long for them unhealthily.
It's much more of a nightmare just being without you now.

Dad And The Heart Shaped Rock

Dad, the heart shaped rock you gave me before you left.
You drove across the country with it to California after the divorce.
You told me you held it in your sweaty hand the entire time. 3,200 miles.
Well, in my immature haste, I gave it away to some girl I don't even talk to now.

Dad, even worse, she kept telling me it was too much for me to give away.
I assured her something insane along the lines of, "He'd want you to have it."
How impulsive can a young man possibly be, right? I'm appalled with myself.
Well, I lost you, AND I lost the heart shaped rock you gave me. I'm so sorry.

And I can't get either back.

Donuts With My Dad

Dad, I went to the donut shop in Sierra Madre.
You know the place; the one you took me to every morning.
Vanilla frosting with rainbow sprinkles for me, and chocolate glazed for you.
I dropped my wallet in front of the Owner and your photo fell out.

"Oh! That's your Dad! How is he? He came in every morning. I haven't seen him lately."
I didn't have the heart to tell him. I didn't have the courage to say it. So, I lied instead.
"Yeah, yeah, um, he's good, good. Just, hasn't been around, you know."
The kind and elderly Owner didn't mean to hurt me, but what he said next destroyed me:

"He makes me laugh every time I see him. He's a good man. You're lucky he's your Father!"

I cried and ate my donuts. I never went back again. But I still have the photo.

I learned after losing your heart shaped rock.

I left a donut for you on the baseball field at Heasley.

A wild, green parrot flew down and scooped it up.

I cried again, and - like always - walked down to my car.

A fatherless boy, a fatherless boy I'll always be.

I'm An Orphan Of This World, But A Child Of God In Heaven

Dear Mama, you died two years ago.
Two years of missing you, Mama.
Two years of questioning myself.
Two years of "Could I have done more?"
Two years of stoicism and conflict.
Two years of two tons of weight.
Two years of feeling like it was yesterday.
Two years of resisting my old lifestyle.
Two years of reading all your emails.
Two years after I spread your ashes in SD.
Two years of starting over without you.
Dear Mama, everyday I hear your words:
"Ry, don't drive down the wrong road."
"Ry, don't let the music stop."
"Ry, don't stop expressing yourself."
"Ry, don't refrain from grieving."
"Ry, don't let them tell you how to hurt."
"Ry, I'm with you when you're alone."
"Ry, I'm the sound inside your drums."
"Ry, I'm the poem that reaches kids."
"Ry, I'm the courage to stay alive."
"Ry, I'm the mountain you bike across."
"Ry, I'm the character you take pride in."
"Ry, I'm with God. You know it's true."
Dear Mama, I quit a real good job.
Dear Mama, I chased my wildest dreams.
Dear Mama, I'm a full-time artist now.

Dear Mama, I DON'T CARE if I go broke.
Dear Mama, I DON'T CARE if I end up rich.
Dear Mama, money has no worth in heaven.
Dear Mama, you said words are powerful.
Dear Mama, I'm telling the world our story.
The story of you, Dad, and I.
The story of the working-class.
The story of the underdogs.
The story of God's Glory.
The story of never losing faith.
The story of never giving up.
The story of ignoring the prognosis.
The story of the last two years.
I miss you, Mama.
I'm telling them all about you.
I won't take this for granted.
The Lord knows what I need.
The Lord tells us not to worry.
The Lord has numbered our days.
And so shall I not need.
And so shall I not want.
And I WON'T take each day for granted.
Even if it costs me my LIFE.
What do I care if I die young?
If I leave this world early,
it's because God sanctioned it.
Therefore, it would be in His will.
Therefore, that's within His purpose.
Therefore, His will over "my own."
Therefore, I'd consider it an HONOR.
CONSIDER ME UNAFRAID.
Until then, every day that I am here -

it is because God ALLOWS me to be.
That means today has PURPOSE.
That means I will WRITE.
I'll write until it kills me.
I'll write 'cause I'm still here.
Two years without you proofreading.
Two years of missing you, Mama.
I'm an orphan without you and Dad.
But I'm a child of the Heavenly Father.
Though He slay me, yet will I trust in Him.

Angelic Birds Of Oregon

Hello, Mama. I miss you.

Mom, it is April 26th.
I replay it all again.
As if I don't on other days.
But I'm replaying it all again.

The guilt of being at work.
The text I got from your husband.
The call I got from him in my car.
The way I could barely breathe.

Mom, it is April 26th.
I've slowed down since then.
I moved to a small town in Oregon.
I finally left Los Angeles.

I am greatly discouraged today.
I shouldn't have seen your dead body.
It traumatized me, though I prayed over it.
It was silly to do that, because you had already left.

Mom, it is the late afternoon of April 26th.
I was supposed to be getting a tattoo in your honor today in Hollywood.
I couldn't fly down because of quarantine.
I stare at the blankness of my arm, where the bird would've been.

You loved birds so much that you'd call me your "Little Chickadee."
Around twenty Yellow Finches rested on my porch today in unison.
I've never seen this happen in the six months I have been here.
It is April 26th, and the birds are here for you. Or, maybe that IS you.

Hello, Mama. I miss you.

My Energy Left When You Did

Mama, I'm so tired even when I'm rested.
I cannot find the stillness that I need.
No matter how much rest I give myself,
I'm still so tired indeed.

It hurt, but I survived.

The Curse Of Dodger Stadium

It was just months before he took his own life.

My Dad pleaded with me to go to a Dodger game with him while I was there.

But, being eighteen, it felt "childish" to me at the time.

I went with my friends instead, and my Dad's feelings were hurt.

I can't believe I did that. I cannot believe that I did that.

I still haven't been able to forgive myself for that.

It's one of my biggest regrets.
I think about it every time I go to a game now.
Every time I walk up Vin Scully Avenue or Stadium Way,
I remember that moment, and I get chills every time.
It's genuine excitement, nostalgia, and a sense that
I am honoring my Dad somehow - by going to games now
as a man - but it's also a longing
that cannot
and will not
ever be fulfilled.
Still, in vain
I continue
to go.

A Grief That Never Subsides

But, back then, we stayed up all night
taking in the moments before
he had to drop me off at the airport.
We sat in his little house
and conversed like dear, old friends.
The lights were off,
and time allowed the windows
throughout the early morning hours
to become gradually filled
with the awakening rays from the sun.
By the time our moments together were complete,
we had to squint from the brightness.
It was the last time I ever saw my Father.

The ATM Machine

I remember him stopping at a Bank Of America
ATM machine in Sierra Madre, just east of Michillinda,
to give me twenty dollars on the way to LAX.
I'm not entirely sure why that's so significant to me.

Actually, that's not true. I dunno why I just said that.

I do know why.

It has nothing to do with money. I think it's because
it was the last thing he did for me as my Father
before he sent me back into "the world."
But, that ATM is still there.
And ... no matter how many years go by,
or how long it's been
since I've driven through the old neighborhood,
I find that my car slows down
every single time I pass it.
I get down to five miles an hour
with the windows down,
with the music off,
and I'm eighteen years old again.
I stay at that speed,
and Dad's just forty-four again.
I hear the calls of wild, green Parrots,
and I see a young man
exiting his vehicle
as he casually jogs across the street
to approach the bank.

I see him pull out his old, brown wallet,
and he then grabs his debit card.
I sit in the front passenger seat
of his ol' red Buick and
I watch him extract a twenty
from the machine.
I watch him jaywalk
back across the street
while he smiles at me
with his eyes.
I feel the pat of his hand
on my left thigh,
while the twenty now rests on it
as he gets back in,
and I hear the door close.
I also hear the "Here you go, Ry,"
with his deep, velvety, painful voice,
as he puts that ol' Buick back into drive.
Boston's "More Than A Feeling" is playing
on his radio as we drive out of Sierra Madre.

Former Best Friend

I tried bro. I TRIED. Are you reading this?
How many conversations did we have?
How many times did I try to express my frustrations to you?
How many times did I try to articulate my growing resentment of you?
How many times did I attempt to save our brotherhood? We were family.
Stop telling our mutual friends you have no idea why I stopped talking to you.
Start taking responsibility for the narcissism and manipulations I walked away from.

Trauma

I have these recurring nightmares
that I am in hospice,
and am dying of Cancer.
I wake myself up
from the petrified whimpers
my voice produces in my sleep.
I cannot catch my breath
'til I've desperately gasped for air
with my lips upon the window screen.
Finally, though deeply disturbed,
I fall asleep after praying to God for protection.

A Thought When A Loved One Dies

I mourn all the things we'll never do together.

Cathartic Cardio

Aimless walks through Franklin Village helped me survive it all.

Turbulence At The Truax's

I remember when Mom threw
a huge set of keys at Dad's face.
They collided with his lower lip and
burst his skin open like a tomato.
I remember when Dad's blood was
dripping all over the kitchen floor.
It was dark red and thick.
He kept dabbing his face with paper towels
and his dress shirt was ruined.
So was the afternoon.
So was our family.
I am still so sad.

Spiritually Hardened

I lost my Grandma.
I lost my Grandpa.
I lost my other Grandma.
I lost my other Grandpa.
I lost my Dad.
I lost my Mom.
What would make you think
that I could not survive
through losing you as well?

An Excruciating Milestone

This year, I'll have been without my Dad

for as many years as I had him.

Half my life without my Father.

A Timeless Declaration

I will say this, though:

I am not a victim.

I am victorious.

My Arms Are Wrapped Around You

My Mother sent me a text message on
January 26th, 2018, exactly four months
before she died. It was one of the last
clear-minded pieces of writing she ever wrote:

"Hi Ry. It's about 1 in the morning
and I hope this doesn't wake you up
and I hope you didn't just
sit home all night crying
please let me know
how you're doing if you're awake.
I know how much you love me,
and I know you love me
with every shred of your being
so please don't be sad
and celebrate the happy times we've had
and the happy times we will continue to make.
We are very blessed.
We are very blessed that
we will have the opportunity
to make more wonderful happy memories
so don't feel sad okay?
I know telling you not to
feel sad isn't very helpful
and it breaks my heart
that you're in pain
and I blame myself.
My own stupid self.
Ryan, nothing and no one

is meant to live forever,
I think that is how God wants it
and we can only accept it
and not fight it.
Just remember, no matter how far
or close apart we are
I will always be your guardian angel
watching over you
and you can always talk to me
whenever you feel the need
and I will hear you
and try to give you answers
and the correct advice.
Thank you for everything.
You are a huge help.
I know it's upsetting for you
when I first wake up.
That's when I'm at my worst
and when the pain is the worst
and I look the worst.
I'm sorry for freaking you out
and I'm not like this all the time.
Let's celebrate the memories
we have made
and will make, Ry.
There are very few
moms and sons
who have what
you and I have,
so we are very lucky.
Nothing can change that
or take that away from us.

So hold onto those thoughts,
as no one can take those thoughts
and memories away from you ever.
We will always have those.
I love you so much.
Let me know how you're doing.
Don't feel sad, okay?
My arms are wrapped around you.
Hugs and kisses, hugs and kisses
Xoxoxoxoxo, mama"

Inquisitive Forms Of Gratitude

How could I be anything but thankful when I've lived a life so rich already?
How could I be angry with all of this tragedy when there is so much beauty?

A Letter To Mom

"Mother, please forgive me for not having
the means to eradicate your hurt -
to uproot the lands of illness,
and to replace it with healthy, nourished soil.
Mother, I pray for you, though admittedly,
I too, am in great need of prayer.
The devil's whispers have manifested into a growl.
He's telling me I am guilty. I am inadequate.
I am not up to par in terms of being
the son that you've always been deserving of.
Forgive me, Mother.
For my heart is dispersed and I am
scrambling to place it back together
so my love for you can be potent enough
to neutralize your pain.
Lord Jesus, may I be graced with
the mannerisms needed
in this impossible circumstance.
May I not be defined or hardened
by the intricacies of this scenario.
Father In Heaven, thank You in that
I feel Your Hand upon the wounds of my soul.
It's gentle, it's tender, and it exudes the equivalency
of the purest aloe vera that's ever been met to
a severe burn in great need of nurturing.
Thank you, God. But forgive me, Mother.
The sight of you writhing in pain is changing me.
Mother, I shall passionately seek to stay unscathed
as this sea of arrows continue to be thrown before me.

I ask our Lord to save you. I ask our Lord to cover you,
for whoever dwells in the shelter of the Most High,
will rest in the shadow of the Almighty.
My dear Mother, how immeasurably have I fallen short
to have lacked the arsenal required to
shift you away from what is seemingly imminent.
Mother, if this causes me to fall back,
I promise that I will make a comeback.
I fear spiritual stagnancy. I crave an affluence in my soul.
My sweet Mother, how gently I cradle you in my dreams.
How thoroughly you are healed and soothed
by the fingertips of the Lord as He bandages your wounds,
as I sleep,
and as I imagine.
Mother, forgive me.
I now not pray for you to heal on this Earth,
but that you are healed up in heaven.
I seek not for you to die,
but for you to LIVE under the comfort
and covering of God's feathers.
I will strive to make sure that you are remembered.
That your suffering wasn't for nothing.
That your journey will inspire millions.
I pray that the Lord graces me with
the honor of being used by Him mightily.
So much so that it cuts my life short.
That it kills me.
I'll die for the Lord.
I'll leave this place
if it means this place
will have been made better
by my humble, little life.

So that you, Mother, will know
that the tiny blonde kid
from Sierra Madre
got off his tricycle,
grew stronger,
and met the opposition of this world
- the darkness -
with confidence,
and in good,
unwavering faith.
Mother, all your illness has done
is make me love you more.
All it has done is make me fall in love
even deeper with our God the Father.
I thank Him on my knees.
Head down, shaky hands raised,
as tears fall and are absorbed by the dirt.
I thank Him for His protection and provision.
His blessing and His grace.
The gift He gave us is our beautiful,
unbreakable connection that shall
supersede human death.
I hope you know how impactful you are
and always will be, sweet Mother.
I hope that I can make you proud.
I hope that you will read this in heaven.
I love you."

—April 25th, 2018, the day before she died.

Mama's Descent Into Dementia

There were no breaks.
Nothing stopped. Ever.
And she never, ever wanted to be alone.
One of us (my Step Dad or I)
always had to be with her,
or she'd throw things, scream, sob,
threaten us, blame us, guilt-trip us, you name it.
Her fiercely strong and charismatic personality
was now
an unrecognizable shadow
of its former self.
She had full-blown dementia,
and she was constantly
on a list of drugs.
The intensity of
her daily drug usage
at this point
was staggering.
It was staggering.

Mama's Daily Regimen

Every day, my Mother had to take 20 mgs of Simvistatin to reduce the possibility of having a heart attack or a stroke.

1 mg of Folic Acid in the avoidance of anemia.

Half a mg of Ipratopium Bromide to keep the airways of her lung passages open.

3 mgs of Albuterol Sulfate to treat inflammation of bronchial tube-lining.

Spiriva Respimat was also ingested to evade bronchospams and chronic obstructive pulmonary disease.

Pro Rescue Inhalers were also habitually used to alleviate breathing hindrances.

1 mg of Ativan (or Lorazepam) was taken 3 times a day, and sometimes every 2 hours if needed. Lorazepam's purpose was to combat anxiety, chemo-induced nausea and vomiting, as well as the prevention of seizures. My Mom was constantly in fear of having a seizure.

100 mgs of Pristiq which was an antidepressant that she was extremely reliant on.

1,200 mgs of Gabapentin every evening for nerve pain and also served as an anticonvulsant.

7.5 mgs of Norco (or Hydrocodone) combined with 325 mgs of Acetaminophen twice a day, sometimes several, or in the middle of the night. This is a potent and powerful painkiller that is highly addictive, and literally can cause respiratory failure and death if irresponsibly used.

30 mgs MS Contin (Morphine) twice a day, once in the morning, and once in the evening. Another powerful source of pain prevention.

Nystatin was an antifungal antibiotic that was taken 2 to 4 times a day in that she was vulnerable to (and an agent of) continuous, varying fungal infections.

4mgs of Dexamethasone (an oral steroid) was taken twice a day to reduce the swelling of her brain dura tumor.

Prilosec was taken midday to combat heartburn.

25 mgs of Hydroxyzine was an Antihistamine taken to treat perpetual itchiness on the body and head.

Ketaconazole cream was applied daily for a foot fungas she had developed which was followed by an anti-itch cream (can't remember the name of that), followed by an application of Vaseline on top of both.

Stenna and stool softeners were taken once a day to help her bowel movements, and sometimes Enemas were required.

.4 mls of Restasis (eye drops) was used once a day to handle chronic dry eye affliction.

1,000 mgs of Calcium, 2,000 units of D-3, and finally, it should be noted that she didn't usually take Advil because,

hey … the doctors didn't want to overdo it.

—Life With Cancer

Ignorance Toward Grief

There's always going to be people
who will judge you in your darkest moment
just because you aren't smiling more.
They don't know what you're facing.
Be serious for as long as
your healing requires you to be.
You owe them nothing.
You do, however, owe yourself.
Don't let anyone rush you.
Walk slowly through the intensity.

Another Father's Day

Another Father's Day without you.
This year, I'm sitting on a porch
in Sun River, Oregon.
I'm drinking coffee I got
from the little town of Sisters.
I'm struck by this thought:
You were so handsome.
Chiseled jawline with style.
A light brown leather jacket.
A white t shirt tucked into jeans.
A pair of boots and a belt.
You owned the 70s and 80s.
No looks and no styles ever matter, though.
You were so broken and so beaten.
Your own Dad stole your identity.
You could never forget or put down
what that sick man did to you.
By the time I was old enough to help,
you had already left.
You and I are like this great
missed encounter or something.
It's like we just barely missed each other.
Had you hung in there a couple more years,
I'd have been old enough to help you.
It kills me that I came back to L.A.
just four months after you died.
Why didn't I move earlier?
I could have led you.
We could've worked out together

and gone to church together
and gone to therapy together
and made friends together
or even lived together.
I just needed a little more time
and maybe I could have saved you.
But you're gone and I've spent
half of my life playing out a fantasy
that will never come to fruition
as I arrogantly act as if
I could have renumbered
the days that God Himself
had predestined for you
in His immensely mysterious wisdom.
And so, I continue to wrestle this grief
that never seems to let up
and I remember how beautiful you were.
I remember your charisma
and your smile and your laugh.
And I am heartbroken that your light
was not enough to protect you
from the darkness that
took you away from me so early.
Your absence is now my darkness,
& I fear I'll ever know light again in this life.
You always told me to change the world.
I'm trying.
But, for the moment,
I sit in Oregon alone and in pain
missing you on another Father's Day.
Like a curse and like a cycle from hell itself,
it's yet another Father's Day without you.

Stigma

Too many men convince themselves to hold back good tears.

—Another Unnecessary Stigma

Harsh Reality

Never rely so little on yourself
that you begin to believe
that there's a single person
on this Earth
that you absolutely
cannot live without.
You might
not WANT to
live without them,
but you COULD
if God took them
earlier than you expected.

One Step At A Time

At the height of my grief,
two men with a guitar
began to joyfully sing
Wonderwall by Oasis
on the street in Barcelona.
I perked up and
I set down my Sangria.
I watched and listened intently.
I even quietly sang along.
Drunk but less depressed,
I eventually made my way
back to my hotel in Spain
feeling encouraged
and truly victorious.

Read Your Mail

Your identity is a carefully written letter

your pain is a tightly sealed envelope

you cannot learn about yourself

until you go through

the tedious process

of opening up.

Cats Of Croatia

Mama always talked about traveling.
She repeatedly mentioned one place in particular.
I forgot the name in my American ignorance.
When she was in hospice, she asked me to go there.
"It's a country where countless cats roam free and are safe."
My Mother adored cats and had many throughout her life.
In my haze and in the emotional moment,
I forgot to write the name of the country down.
After she passed, and after her funeral,
I planned a trip to Europe as I promised her I'd do.
Ireland. Italy. Spain. France.
I couldn't wait. But I had time for one more country.
Out of nowhere, H-Bear had an idea:
"My Dad says Croatia is gorgeous. What about going there?"
I looked it up and indeed it was a beautiful place.
I knew so little about the country and I liked that.
I wanted to explore. I wanted to try new things.
So, I booked a flight to Dubrovnik.
When I arrived, my Step-Dad text me:
"Hi Ry, how are you? Where are you at now?"
"Hey man, I flew out of Paris and just landed in Croatia."
He immediately replied, "YES! You got to visit it for her!"
Confused, I responded, "What? What do you mean?"
"Your Mother, Ry. Croatia. The cats are in Croatia."
My shaky hand could not reply.
My face was soaked in tears.
I sat on the rocks of Sunset Beach in Dubrovnik and sobbed.
I involuntarily rocked back and forth from all the pain.
But, much to my delight, I looked up through the tears and noticed.

There were black and white Croatian cats roaming everywhere.
Locals treated them with sincere respect.
Food was outside for them everywhere.
All the cats were sweet and friendly.
The cats of Croatia aren't afraid of us.
The cats of Croatia sit on your lap in restaurants.
The cats of Croatia are a part of Dubrovnik's gorgeous culture.
The cats of Croatia are what my Mama asked me to see.
And in my Mama's death she made it happen.
And in my Mama's life she made me happy.
And in my all-consuming, debilitating grief,
I was surrounded by all the cats of Croatia.

Loss

At my most honest,
I'm just a little boy who
misses his Mommy & Daddy.
Through all my painful loss, though,
I was never, ever abandoned by God.
God gave me this beautiful thing called life.

Life

I Am Trying To Forgive You All

We held different funerals for my Dad.
You didn't call me when he was dying.
Why - at 18 - did I have to call you guys?
I heard you tried to blame it on his job.
I heard you tried to extort the company.
"You're gonna have to send us money."
My Dad's friend overheard the phone call.
The phone call you made in the hospital.
The call you chose to make instead of calling me.
Was that all his suicide was to you guys?
A transactional opportunity to get money?
And how dare you blame my Mother.
You don't know what happened.
You're all completely clueless.
My Grandfather molested my Dad.
Do you care to know that?
My Dad was given demons.
My Dad then beat my Mother.
His Dad opened up darkness.
But you blame my Mom?
Who forced my Dad to jump?
Who forced him off that bridge?
Why don't you call his Shrink?
Dad was on and off his meds.
You should blame the meds.
You should blame his demons.
You should blame depression.
You should blame his Father.
But don't ever blame my Mother.

My Mom endured my Dad's abuse.
How dare you judge her because she left.
None of you ever talk about my Dad.
No photos of him or anything.
It's conveniently like he never existed.
You all have cookouts together and laugh.
I'm just the kid from L.A. that nobody ever talks about.
But I'm talking to you now. And - I am trying to forgive you all.

You're All My Father's Friends

I know you think I'm angry.
I know *you're* probably angry.
I know your friend was "Alan" to you.
I know your friend was "Dad" to me.

So, let's debunk all the *defensiveness*:
Yes, he was a good Father in many ways.
Yes, he encouraged me to be an artist.
Yes, he watched every game I ever played.
Yes, he had a room *just* for all my trophies.

But, let's debunk all the *perceptions*:
No, he wasn't as balanced as you assert him to be.
No, he wasn't as kind as you claim he habitually was.
No, he wasn't as joyful behind the curtains of our home.
No, he wasn't capable of telling you the entire story.

My writing was *never* meant to depict my Father poorly.
My writing was *never* meant to imply that he was a bad man.
My writing was *never* meant to make you all despise me.
My writing was *never* meant to hurt any of you.

Please, let's debunk all of the *stigmas*:
Can't a young man love his Dad yet *take issue* with him?
Can't a young man be angry that his Dad *took his own life?*
Can't a young man feel *unresolved* while lacking closure?
Can't a young man *express* his pain, while *loving his Father*, too?

Edward - my Father said you rescued him every day from his drunk parents. *Thank you.*

Jason - my Father said you continuously made him laugh no matter what. *Thank you.*

Ben - my Father adored you and you were the last person to see him alive. *Thank you.*

Mark - my Father's greatest joy was swimming in Lake Champlain with you. *Thank you.*

Chris - my Father idolized you. I don't know where you are. But I miss you. *Thank you.*

You five, along with all his other friends *must know this:* You were his brightness in the dark.

You five, along with all his other friends *must know this:* He laughed his hardest with you.

You five, along with all his other friends *must know this:* Your acceptance of him was precious.

You five, along with all his other friends *must know this:* You taught me so much about him.

You five, along with all his other friends *must know this:* You were all he ever really had.

After all, you're *all* immensely special. After all, *you're all my Father's friends.*

Self-Sufficiency

I am by myself,

but I am not alone.

Crying Is For The Strong

Crying shouldn't be forbidden.
Expression must be had.
Emotion is a necessity.
Bawling builds backbone.
Weeping is wealthiness.
Wisdom oozes through tears.

The Mind Of an Addict

When an addict won't
rejoice for your sobriety,
it does not stem from
a lack of support or selfishness.
It is because your liberation holds
a magnifying glass up to the prison bars
they still continue to sit behind,
and they are therefore unable to see
the great outdoors of your recovery.

Courage

Oh, c'mon.
I'm going to get judged either way.
I'd rather it be for what I bravely expressed
instead of what I fearfully kept to myself.

Closure In Simply Leaving

I never got an apology
for all the abuse
but I pardoned
myself form it
and I will heal

Understanding Panic Attacks

Having some anxiety
does not mean you're insane.
Having no compassion for it
— however —
is absolutely crazy.

Cowards

Bullies don't think about
why they hurt you,
they just want to
forget about
their pain.

Gravestone Of Immaturity

In loving memory
of my old self.
It is survived by
the desire within me to mature.

Learning Takes Longer

I could wrongly answer you now,
or I could correctly answer you later.
For foolishness is at your feet,
but wisdom is in the wilderness.

Don't Compare Journeys

They're not ahead of you.
They just started before you.
They have past achievements,
but you have future accomplishments.

Unraveling The Woman

A confident woman
won't tear another
woman down.
A respectable woman
isn't enticed by men
who objectify her.
A wise woman
won't lash out at
those who never
wronged her
to begin with.
Any woman
-however-
can rise
above
it all.

Unpacking The Man

A confident man
will want you
to succeed.
An insecure man
will feel threatened
when you thrive.
An angry man
falls prey to his
venomous emotion.
A sensitive man
is often quite offended.
Any man -however-
can change with
accountability.

Never Give Up

Do Not Give Up, Okay?
Discover new friends.
Avoid shady people.
Set down the bottle.
Put down the pills.
Stop self-harming.
Stop self-shaming.
Stop eating poorly.
Get up a bit earlier.
Go for a long walk.
Listen to podcasts.
Learn information.
Discuss your pain.
Read more books.
Save your money.
Drink more water.
Get ample sleep.
Explore hobbies.
Find community.
Let go of anger.
Respect others.
Don't be alone.
Stay optimistic.
Exercise more.
Forgive more.
Listen more.
Smile more.
Give more.
Be real.
Love.

The Power Of Your Voice

The world is a microphone,
and it's pointing
directly at you.
Walk up to it
and speak.

A Moment Of Honesty

It's not just you.
We ALL have
insecurities.

The Will To Chase Your Dreams

Friends, do not lay upon your death bed
having passively wandered through living.
Do not recall decades of wasted years
and find yourself overcome with regret.
Take many leaps of faith.
Take a lot of risky chances.
Smile as failure stares you down.
Find the will to chase your dreams.
Don't get caught dancing with indifference.
Pursue the rhythms of enthusiasm.
Watch it and learn its movements.
Then, dance with that instead.
If appreciation is a waterfall,
then you should stand beneath it.
Soak yourself in its beauty
until you're drenched in life.
Make sure the ground runs below you
before a gravestone rests above you.
Find the will to chase your dreams.

Hypocrisy

You have all these demands of people,
yet you never uphold yourself
to the same standard
you push upon their
every single move.

Spiritual Conductor

Leadership is orchestration.
But do you have the charisma
to assemble enough musicians?

A Hasty Appetite

The cafe on Hollywood and Wilton is overpriced,
but their breakfast burritos are life-changing.
Therefore, I am broke.

Rhythmic Restlessness

*I play drums because
it's the closest thing to
the sound of my soul
that I can conjure up.*

A Leather Lining

When I had that gun to my head, I was thankful.
He took my iPhone, my debit card and my driver's license.
What he didn't take was my Schott leather jacket —
which was the only thing that couldn't be replaced.

Nowhere Else To Go

I used to skate at this dilapidated park off of Wilton and Fountain.
You had to jump two fences to get in, but if you got in,
the ramps and the rails were glorious.
Made me feel like the kid I was
before I lost my family.
As a grown man,
I'd skate around and
daydream about my childhood
until a security guard would come
and ask me to leave. I'd leave so sad again.

Communicative Restraint

You don't always need to have the last word.

Ally Or An Enemy

You're either fighting against racism
or you're contributing TO racism.
There are no sidelines here.
You're on one side of the
battlefield or the other.

I'm Calling You Out

You're disturbed you're not in shape,
but you're complacent
without exercising.
Why is that?

Unapologetically

It amazes me that poets
who share their work on social media,
are seen as "inferior" or "less credible"
to a certain demographic of individuals,
solely based on the fact that they
use these platforms to connect with readers.
I respect an individual's freedom
to dislike an artist's actual work.
What I don't respect is
disliking an artist's work
because of the ways
they are trying to get their art
to be seen by a larger audience.
I'll plaster my words to a toaster
if it means more people will read them
while they make their breakfast.

I'll share my words
through letters,
through emails,
through smoke signals,
through paper airplanes,
or through social media
if I think that it will
connect with a kid out there
and will encourage them
in their journey.
Artists, share your work EVERYWHERE.

Unapologetically.
I apologize for nothing.

The Men Up Mulholland Drive

Three powerful men in the Hollywood industry
sexually harassed and assaulted me when I was 25.
One of them pulled out his checkbook
and asked, "How much to see your dick?"
I left his mansion crying.
I actually thought they believed in me.
They're all still living successful lives.
Nothing was ever done.
Only one of them "apologized,"
but even he just casually blamed the booze.

—My Soul Still Hurts

Codependency

You expect me to listen to your problems
and you treat me like I'm your therapist,
yet with all the talking about yourself
that you find the time to do,
you never make time to ask
how I might be feeling
or how I might be doing.
And as the cycle continues,
everything is always about you,
and you don't even realize it.
But here you are, judging me-
'cause I'm finally impatient with listening-
'cause I'm finally drained by your self-centeredness.

Laziness

The sacrifices it takes
to truly pursue your dreams
are far too time-consuming
and far too costly
for most individuals
to remain committed to.
These are the same people
who sit around with their
unmanaged time and wonder
why they haven't made a million dollars
without realizing that
they haven't made an effort
worth more than a hundred pennies.

Receptiveness

The quickest way
to stay the same
and to never grow
is through lacking accountability.
You want to grow and progress?

Learn how to handle criticism.

You Don't Have To Do This Alone

My Dear, Beloved Friend -
I love you. I LOVE you.
Don't you see that I am HERE?
I can't let you close that door.
Don't you see the sun outside?
You're in an unimaginable form of pain.
Could you take one more shaking step?
You're in an excruciatingly lonely place.
Could you make one more loving friend?
You feel like it's so dark outside.
Don't you see that morning's come?
I can't let you close your book.
Don't you see more chapters there?
I'm not the only one who loves you.
WE love you. We LOVE you.
Don't you see that we are here?
We can't let you give up now.
Don't you see your soul is kind?
You're filled with blinding self-hatred.
Could you take any one of our hands?
You're surrounded by outstretched arms.
Don't believe the lie that you're alone.
Don't give in to the piercing impulses.
Let's just cry together - you know?
Let's just VENT about it - okay?
Let's just PAUSE a moment - yes?
Let's just bare our burdens - please?
I am IN THIS with you.
We ALL are, dear friend.

I'm right here. Feel my hand.
It's warm and alive for you.
And they're waiting outside to help.
They're patiently waiting for you.
No one is burdened by you at all.
There's definitely no one annoyed.
No one is pressed for time, either.
There's nobody laughing at you here.
The priority for everyone is YOU.
You don't have to give up.
You can make it further.
You could heal and thrive.
You don't have to do this alone.
Can you please try to see us?
We can SEE you, dear friend.
Just stay right there.
Don't let go.
We can REACH YOU.
We're coming to get you.
Just don't let go.
We all love you. We ALL love you.
God is an intravenous drip.
Let Him fill all your veins.
You don't have to do this alone.

If I Die, Here's What I Meant

I want you all to remember me in my rawest form.
Recall me in my absolute, most vibrant prime.
Downtrodden but joyful, optimistic yet cynical,
driving down Sunset Blvd. Remember me like this:
Chasing moments that will make me feel deeply alive.
Ray-Ban sunglasses on, you know - the original
Tortoise shell-Wayfarer classic pair that I love.
Picture me tan, lean, scruffy-faced, with a white T-shirt,
blue jeans, converse, while my dirty blonde hair
gets combed by the weekend wind as
Lana Del Rey's "Born To Die" drowns the pain out.
Schott leather jacket laying in the back seat.
Bandaged forearms while the tattoos heal that
Asa had recently inked on me at Shamrock.
Remember me leaving Dayglow with a fresh n' gorgeous cup.
Driving away from my filthy, eastern Hollywood neighborhood.
Remember me driving past Amoeba toward Bel Air.
Away from the pain of loss, and all I've been forced to overcome.
But remember me in the best shape of my life,
smiling while I drive as I reminisce about all the people
who swore that I'd never, ever get off all the drugs.
Remember me as a young man from Southern California -
the common tale of a musician who came from a broken home -
who drove through the prettiest parts of the city -
scheming and plotting as to how some insignificant, working-class kid
could possibly become a part of the glory within Los Angeles.
Remember my favorite city, and remember that my favorite moments
were when I'd put off all my errands to drive down Sunset Blvd.
Chasing elusive emotions that

for a split second would make me feel alive
'til I'm dumped out onto the Pacific Coast Highway.
Remember me laying in the sands of Malibu.
Remember me procrastinating from returning to
the grimy intersection of Hollywood and Western.
But remember that I kept coming back,
I kept withstanding punches,
and that I survived despite it all.
I survived though I felt completely alone.
But I was never alone for a second.
For God was perpetually present.
For the glory goes all to God.
For God gave my life a meaning.
And if I die, this is what it meant.

—A Eulogy For Myself

Life

With all the life I've lived,
and all the things I've experienced,
all of it would be completely meaningless
if I didn't have my Heavenly Father in Heaven.
My perfect and my glorious, never-changing Lord.

Lord

He, And He Only

God is the only one
who can increase
your faith
and decrease
your fear.

Savior Of Sinners

First time I ever went to Church,
I ran back to my car in tears and
I fearfully drove home in shame.
But God wasn't done with me.

Mustard Seed

Many are our doubts,
but few are our beliefs.

Reverse the ratio.

Church Culture

They'll encourage you in your faith.
They'll say that God will regenerate.
Regeneration is messy, though.
So, many congregants will panic.
And to supplement their discomfort,
some of them will slander you.
Beware, for the individuals who
encouraged your repentance
are the same ones who
discourage your spiritual imperfections.
Therefore, the strong recipients become angry,
and the meek recipients become absent.
But, they'll "encourage" you in your faith.

Disclaimer: Not all believers are like this.
Another disclaimer: Too many are.

Satanism In The Entertainment Industry

The Devil's approach is subtle.
He surrounds us in his presence gradually.
The Devil does this through demonic imagery.
He surrounds us in his intelligent lies.
The Devil won't come at you blatantly.
He surrounds you with beautiful songs.
The Devil will give you what you want.
He surrounds you with all you don't need.

Psych Ward

I did too many drugs,
and had a mental breakdown.
I hallucinated for days,
and they sent me to the ward.
I was in there for almost two weeks,
and my "friends" all called me crazy.
I saw kids permanently lose their minds,
and God alone preserved my sanity.

Premonitions

The Calvanists would reject them.
The Charismatics would construe them.
Is there an in-between?
Or do dreams mean not a thing?
Are you a continuationist?
Or are you a cessationist?
Research these things.

Another Day

God, some days I get so severely tired.
I just cannot imagine going forward.
And I have no clue how to do it.
But this morning came.
And I woke up.
Thank you.
I'll try.

70 X 7

We must forgive one another
despite a world so racked with
vengeance, war, and rage.

Appreciate It *Before* It's Gone

If Death had a gravestone,
upon its surface it would read:
From dust you were created.
To dust you'll become again.
Before your parents die.
Before your relationship ends.
Before your friends grow apart.
Appreciate these people now.
Before your mind slows down.
Before your body's health declines.
Before your energy depletes.
Appreciate your youth now.
Before the winter returns.
Before the temperature drops.
Before the clouds congregate.
Appreciate sunny days now.
Before the libraries are gone.
Before the music stores close down.
Before the museums lose relevance.
Appreciate beautiful art now.
Before hardship persists.
Before tragedy arrives.
Before trials befall you.
Appreciate God now.
Before it gets bad, love that it's easy.
Before it gets dark, stare into brightness.
Before it gets lonely, engage with your peers.
Appreciate it before it's gone.
From dust you were created.
To dust you'll become again.

Honest Hearts Hold Humility.

Do not exalt yourself.
Be clothed in humility.
Love mercy and act justly.
With pride comes disgrace.
Wisely listen to advice.
Arrogance foreshadows your downfall.
Humility comes before honor.
Self-praise should never leave your lips.
Live harmoniously with your neighbors.
Value others above your own self.
Never act as if you know tomorrow's fate.
You are a mist that shall soon vanish.
Passionately evade the act of boasting.
Delight in obedience.
Reject all rebellion.
Beauty is that of your inner self.
A quiet, gentle spirit has unfading beauty.
Never announce when you give to the needy.
Be sympathetic.
Be compassionate.
Be honest.
Be humble.
Friend, may I ask you -
In what way do you hold yourself?
With pride? Or with humility?
Ask yourself this -
"Have I honestly humbled myself?"
Honest hearts hold humility.
God adorns the afflicted.

Praise In The Midst Of Hardship

The plants my Mom would tend to on the porch have all withered.
There is no food in the bird feeder, and there are no more hummingbirds.
There is nothing in this place but dust, trash bags, boxes,
and the reminder that despite my entire family all being gone,
despite them having all left this Earth,
God will never leave me for as long as I am on it.

—*Never Lose Faith*

The Struggle With Pornography

Dear God, I'm evil.
I did it yet again.
I knew I was going to.
I felt the desire but I ...
I didn't fight hard enough.
I didn't push it down.
Or maybe I didn't pull it out?
Or maybe I tried to hide it?
What did I do wrong?
Because HERE I AM AGAIN.
Ashamed.
Dirty.
Filthy.
Unworthy.
Another day of sin.
Another day of ugliness.
I did better for a while, yeah.
I didn't do it for a while, YEAH.
But I've been doing it every day.
And my excuses are usually:
"But I'm not having sex."
"But I'm not sleeping around."
"But I'm not being intimate."
"But I hate it afterward."
But do I REALLY?
Because I keep coming back to it,
and I keep turning my back on YOU.
Yet, you never turn on me.
And I wonder, God -

Will your patience ever run out?
Will I have finally abused
your grace enough times?
Will you finally cast me away?
Down with the brimstone?
Down with the teeth-gnashers?
Am I like Esau? Incapable of
real, repentant tears?
Am I too corrupted?
Have I been too hardened?
Kill me now if so, Lord,
so that I may not go on
recklessly rebelling against you.
But please, Jesus -
Could you please remember me?
So that I may dwell with You
inside of your Kingdom?
May I join the thief on the cross
as I am no cleaner than he was
but still You assured him that
on that very day -
he'd be with You in Paradise?
I'd rather be a thief and with You,
than a so-called good man
and in hell. So, please take me.
I'm tired of my flesh.
I'm tired of living down here.
I want to be sanctified and with You.
Because I did it yet again.
I knew I was going to.
I'm evil.

Christian Masturbation

The release clears my mind and
unburdens me of the lustful thoughts.
These thoughts clutter my mind and
my decision-making unless I submit to them.
I'm no longer sleeping around but
even conversing with women is more than
I am equipped to safely handle
without fantasizing about them.
Not having sex with my girlfriend is
an accomplishment I never thought I'd achieve.
I have nowhere to direct this
sexual frustration and tension, God.
Am I some depraved creep?
People have NO IDEA
how difficult this is for me.
Am I a total FAKE? I go to church,
I read the Bible, I pray and
I praise You, God.
I praise You both in private
and in public, and I don't
shy away from the truth.
Yet I cannot go
a single day without masturbating.
I cannot go a single day without
releasing the sexual tension.
Pastors have said not all men struggle with this.
The Calvinists rip on men like me.
I am scum to them.
Is calling it a "struggle" just a cop out?

Is this my decision, God?
Am I just choosing to do dark things?
Then why do I lay awake at night?
Hating my very core and
questioning my salvation?
I'm tired of questioning the
legitimacy of my salvation.
Can I find no joy in the
presence of your Holy Spirit?
Are my iniquities too crimson to blot out?
Am I too filled with transgressions
to be one of your chosen ones?
Everyone tells me not to strive.
I don't WANT to strive.
I've prayed to You
to change my desires.
I've admitted to You
that I LOVE lust.
I LOVE women.
I LOVE kinky, passionate sex.
I LOSE myself in the THOUGHT of it.
Can you please redeem me, Lord?
How contrite could I possibly be when
I come to You and run to You daily?
Every.
Single.
Day.
With the same old sin and
my same old habits?
Do I love masturbation
more than Jesus?
The Bible says that You will not

allow me to be tempted
beyond what I am able to escape
and to bear, yet I am IMPRISONED
and it's unbearable. I take the blame.
I hold You accountable for nothing.
But as I've prayed for years -
can You please change me God?
I've stopped sleeping around.
I've stopped looking at porn.
Well, mostly.
Sometimes I fall into porn for a week
or so and then you pull me back out.
But I've come so far and all because of You.
Can you please eradicate these roots as well?
I'm a Christian who masturbates daily.
Am I even saved?
I'm so tired of feeling unsafe not in this life,
but in the life to come.
Jesus said to fear not the One
who can kill the body.
He said to be afraid of the One
who can destroy both soul and body in hell.
I don't WANT to sin against you,
yet I love it in the moment.
I have studied Psalm 51.
I have listened to sermons.
I have prayed.
I've studied true repentance for years -
trying to embody it.
I HATE my flesh. I HATE my sin.
I am hopeless and I am broken.
Yet as Paul says, I do the things I hate

and not the things I love.
I just love You, God.
Can You please change me?
I NEED YOU.
I HAVE NOTHING AND
AM NOTHING WITHOUT YOU, GOD.
OUT OF THE DEPTHS,
I HAVE CRIED UNTO THEE.

Repentance

Sin always exhausts me.
Obedience always refreshens me.

Little Tony

God taught me many lessons through little Tony.

He was tiny and very thin.
He had big, brown eyes.
He had big, huge glasses.
He was in 3rd grade and I was in 4th.
His sister was in my class as well.
His sister told me he idolized me.
His sister said he wanted to be like me.
His sister asked me to go talk to him.
My friends bullied Tony a lot.
My friends thought he was a runt.
My friends made fun of his silly, boundless smile.
My friends never let him on the playground.
I always hated myself for saying nothing.
I always hated myself for staying neutral.
I always said hello to him in private.
I always acted above him in public.
Even still, little Tony joyfully approached me one day.
Even still, little Tony courageously walked onto the soccer field.
Even still, little Tony stopped that damn game in the middle of its tracks.
Even still, little Tony pulled out a dull pencil and a crumpled sheet of paper.
"Um, excuse me, Ryan? Can I have your autograph?"
"What? Why would you want my autograph?"
He smiled, shrugged and simply said, "'Cause you're cool."
I smiled, shrugged and simply replied, "Okay, Tony. Sure."
And all my friends made fun of him as he gleefully skipped away.
And all his sister's friends made fun of him as well.
And all little Tony wanted was my autograph.
And all I could think back then is what I still think right now:

The world does not deserve a sweet but giant soul like "little" Tony.
He wasn't little at all.
He was bigger than all of us.

I look up to him to this very day.
I learned so much from Tony.

God puts giant spirits into tiny bodies.

A Letter To God

She's so near death.
There's fear in her confused eyes.
Her shoulders look like elbows.
Her palms are ICE cold.
Held her hand per usual but this time
it was like gripping ice cubes. I am insane.
This has caused me to lose my mind.
The only thing that is making me want to live is God.
And knowing that He will carry me through this.

My Mom doesn't know what year it is.
We had to re-explain to her that her Father died,
my Father died, her dogs have all died years ago.
Her perception of time is as lost as I am at this moment.
Nothing has sunken in yet but I am bleeding internally.
Rapidly. The vitals in my soul are depleting. In vain,
I am trying to seal an array of psychological lacerations
that are spurting streams of deep, dark, red blood
with tiny, petty cotton balls, paperthin napkins,
and generic-brand gauze. It is useless, it is fruitless.
I am gushing with despair. I am stuck to this scenario
like gooey, melted, summer tar. I am unable to break away,
and the heat of this circumstance is so close to my face.
My skin's about to blister, boil, and open.
Jesus, please drench me as
YOU are the only fountain
that could ever bring me relief.
I'm over here
feeling like I'm gonna die,
but still I am worshipping you.

I couldn't go to church this Sunday, God.
Please forgive me. How contradictory of my faith
to have pulled back in the exact moment that
I should have pressed in. But I couldn't be seen
with these pain-filled, dilated eyes. I am so transparent.
I can't explain and re-explain everything to my friends
and acquaintances, nor can I pretend like
I am fine around them either. I am desperate
to emulate Your posture, and Your posture alone, Jesus.

Lord, the enemy is encouraging me to isolate myself.
The enemy is entering this storm and is raking his
sharp nails down the sails on my boat.
The fabric is ripped, the seams are frayed and perforated,
and the freezing air is bursting
through the centers of my resilience
with relentless aggression. My tears are being met
with the devil's contentment and satisfaction.
I wince and satan relishes every moment.

But I know you've not left me here for good, Father!
The sails are torn and my heart is broken,
but this ship is STILL afloat
and my heart is STILL beating.
That means You aren't finished with me yet.
And if You aren't through,
then how could I ever possibly give up?
THIRTY-THREE days since my mother has eaten food
and STILL she hangs on. STILL she lingers.
She fears you, Lord. She fears where she is going.
And as you know, weeks ago she
outstretched her little hands to you, God.

Just like she did when she was healthier.
But this time, instead of saying it
with clear annunciation, she clumsily slurred
out the name of your Son. She begged you,
pleaded to you for forgiveness for
a LIFETIME of sin in the midst of
the haze and darkness in that room.
It's a stale, sick room that always has
the lights off, and has always had these
pointless reruns looping on the television.
However, as it could be felt in ANY tent,
I felt the Holy Spirit in that space.
And while my feelings mean nothing and
your Word means EVERYTHING, forgive me
as I try not to embellish on just
how PRESENT you were at that moment.

I prayed time and time again
for you to save my Mother, Lord.
Like the thief on the cross,
my Mother turned her head to You
and said, "Remember me, Lord."

And now the enemy is seething in
my ear like a rabid snake.
He alleges You didn't hear her words
and that my precious Mother will be
dragged to the sulfur and brimstone
with the rest of the unsanctified.
But I DON'T BELIEVE IT, Lord.
As Jesus replied to the devil with Scripture,
SO WILL I. For your WORD says that

The LORD is CLOSE to the brokenhearted
and SAVES THOSE WHO ARE CRUSHED IN SPIRIT.
And for that I am on my KNEES, Jesus.
Not in front of anyone, not for them,
not for what anyone says, but for YOU.
Because when I pray, I go into my room,
close the door and I pray to YOU, Father.
And You, my Father who sees what is done in secret,
will reward me. HOWEVER, I worship you NOT
for tokens of appreciation, God! I worship You
because YOU are the KING of Kings and the LORD or Lords.
It is YOU, Jesus, who loves me and RELEASED me
from my sin by the power of Your BLOOD. And so
I give THANKS to you, Lord. For You are GOOD,
and Your love endures forever and ever. Amen."

—April 25th, 2018, the day before she died.

Black Magic

I will never fear
your black magic
for the Holy Spirit
that dwells within me
is an impenetrable
hedge of protection
that you too
can receive
if you'd just
give up on
that nonsense
and believe in
the only One
who can truly
save you.
His name
is Jesus.

Current Christianity

Many Pastors of today
distort true Scripture.
The true God of the Bible
does not value our health,
He does not value our success,
He does not value our comfort -
or even our happiness -
in the way that these Pastors
claim that God allegedly does.
The sobering truth is this:
Jesus did not save us from
illness, failure, or sadness.
He saved us from God Himself
in that His wrath was upon us
due to our literal inability
to save ourselves
no matter how "good"
we try to claim we are.
None of us are good. No, not one.
God's standard of "good" is
thoroughly incomprehensible
to any and every human being.
The American "Gospel" is diluted.
Many current "Christians" of today
couldn't explain the Gospel to you
if you asked them to. Hear my heart.
This is not to sound legalistic.
This is not to sound works-based.
This is not to behave like a Pharisee.

I am THE sinner of all sinners.
This is a sincere plea
in defense of the Gospel.
Much of this responsibility
rests on the shoulders of
our Christian leaders.
We MUST DO BETTER.
Many Pastors of today
distort true Scripture
in fear of offending
a carnal world
and that is the state
of current "Christianity."

38

If I die really young,

at some early age like 38,

just know that I was blessed.

Glory goes all to God.

He gave me a thought.

He gave me a hand.

He gave me a pen.

He gave me a paper.

I got to write about it all.

And, I meant every word.

Lord

With love
shall come loss.
With loss
shall come life.
With life
shall come the Lord.
Love, loss, and life
are filled with such beauty.
But the Lord's beauty
supersedes the best of
all that love, loss and life
could ever bring us on this Earth.
Live for the Lord, no matter how difficult.
When we die, all that will have any meaning
will always and only be Him. And so, dear friend,
I say to you simply this: May you never lose your faith.
And if you die, may you have known what all of this meant.

—Ry